A Discovery Biography

Dorothea L. Dix

—◆—

Hospital Founder

by Mary Malone
illustrated by Katharine Sampson

CHELSEA JUNIORS
A division of Chelsea House Publishers
New York ◆ Philadelphia

The Discovery Biographies have been prepared under the
educational supervision of Mary C. Austin, Ed.D.,
Reading Specialist and Professor of Education, Case
Western Reserve University.

Cover illustration: Bruce Weinstock

First Chelsea House edition 1991

1 3 5 7 9 8 6 4 2

ISBN 0-7910-1436-3

Contents

Dorothea L. Dix
Hospital Founder

Chapter *1*

Orange Court

Seven-year-old Dorothea Dix walked about the garden at Orange Court, smelling the lovely spring flowers. She always felt happy here at her grandparents' home in Boston.

Suddenly she stopped. Her grandfather, Dr. Elijah Dix, hurried from the big, red brick house. His carriage was waiting in the driveway.

Dorothea ran over to him. "Grandfather, may I go with you?"

His eyes twinkled. "Is that why you are all dressed up, Dolly?"

She shook her head. "No. Grandmother said my old clothes were ragged."

Every time Dorothea came to Orange Court, the same thing happened. A maid scrubbed her and helped her put on new clothes. Then Dorothea went to her Grandmother. "Now," Grandmother said, "you look like my namesake."

Grandfather Dix was rich and successful. But his son, Dorothea's father, was a failure. At nineteen, Joseph Dix had left Harvard College to get married. Then he and his wife moved from Boston to southern Maine. They lived in a little village called Hampden.

Dorothea was born in 1802, in a one-room, tumble-down cottage. Four years later, her brother Joseph was born, and then Charles. Mr. Dix was nervous and moody. He seldom kept a job for long.

The family would have been hungry if Grandfather had not helped. Mrs. Dix was sickly and was always complaining about her health. Neither she nor Mr. Dix showed much love for their children. Dorothea was the one who really looked after the little boys.

Sometimes Dr. Dix came to see them, and took Dorothea to Boston for a visit. At Orange Court, she had a room of her own and time to play. Best of all, she had Grandfather. No matter how busy he was, he always found time for her.

He had taught her to read from the books in his library.

Now she slipped her hand in his. "Please take me with you."

Dr. Dix nodded. "I will, if you won't get tired. I have a great many patients to visit."

One afternoon they were on the way home. "You will have to go back to Hampden tomorrow, Dolly," he said. "Your mother has sent for you."

"Oh, Grandfather!" she cried. "Why can't I live with you?"

"I wish you could, Dolly. But your Grandmother says she is too old to start raising another family. If we were to keep you here, we'd have to send for your brothers too. They could not get along in Hampden without you."

"But I would look after them here," Dorothea said. "I'll tell Grandmother that."

Soon Grandfather's carriage stopped in front of Orange Court. Dorothea went to look for Grandmother. She opened the parlor door without knocking.

Grandmother was having tea with her sister, Sarah Duncan.

Madam Dix, as the doctor's wife was known in Boston, looked up. "Dorothea! Where are your manners?"

"I'm sorry, Grandmother," Dorothea began, "but . . . ."

"You must learn better," Grandmother said. "Please go to your room."

Unhappily, the girl went upstairs. She had lost her chance to ask about staying at Orange Court.

Chapter 2

Home in Hampden

The next morning, Grandfather put Dorothea on the stagecoach for Hampden. No one met her there. Alone she walked down a muddy lane to her home.

Her three-year-old brother Joseph was playing outside the Dix cottage. "Dolly!" he cried happily.

Dorothea hugged him hard. Then she hurried inside to see the baby. Little Charles, too, smiled happily when he saw his sister.

14

"Is that you, Dorothea?" Her mother's voice came from a bed in a dim corner of the room.

"Yes, Mother. I'm back."

Mrs. Dix sighed. "You'll have to feed the little ones. I'm too tired."

She did not ask about Dorothea's visit.

Dorothea's father was not home. Joseph Dix had failed at farming and selling books. Now he had become a preacher. He was doing better, but he was away for days at a time. He had to ride miles into the backwoods where there were no regular ministers.

He was away when a letter from Boston came for him, several weeks later. When he returned, Dorothea gave him the letter. She waited expectantly for the news from Orange Court.

Her father's face told her that something was wrong. "My father is dead," he said, turning away.

Dorothea's eyes filled with tears. "I will never see Grandfather again!" she sobbed.

As she grew older, life became even harder for Dorothea. Her happiness at Orange Court was only a memory. At Hampden, she did most of the housework. She hauled water, built fires, and weeded the garden. She also helped her father with his work. He had copies of his sermons printed. Dorothea sewed the pages together so he could sell them.

She taught her brothers to read and write, as Grandfather Dix had taught her. She wished she could go to school so that she could learn more.

"Mother, may I go to school this year?" she asked every fall when school opened.

"Girls should stay home," Mrs. Dix said.

When she was twelve, Dorothea decided to leave Hampden. She told her brothers first.

"I am going to Boston, to live with Grandmother," she said. "*She* will let me go to school."

Little Charles began to cry. "Don't go, Dolly! Who will take care of me?"

Dorothea put her arms around him. "Mother and Joseph will manage," she said. "And I will send for you as soon as I can."

"Are you sure Grandmother will take you?" Joseph asked.

"Of course," Dorothea said confidently. To herself, she added, "She must."

"But what will Father say?" Joseph continued.

"If he says no, I'll run away!" she declared.

Dorothea's father did not want her to leave. However, she asked so often that finally he let her go.

Chapter *3*

From Boston to Worcester

Madam Dix was glad to see her granddaughter, for she had been lonely since Dr. Dix died. She nodded when Dorothea told her about leaving home. "Yes, it is time you learned how to be a lady. You are a Dix, and should make a good marriage, as I did."

"But I would like to go to school, Grandmother," Dorothea said.

"Of course," Grandmother said.

She sent Dorothea to the best private school in Boston. The girl became a very good student. She enjoyed books and learning.

However, she did not like the household tasks that Grandmother gave her.

"Learning to sew and to cook are part of your education," Madam Dix said.

Dorothea did not think so. She was careless about her clothes and was often late for meals.

Madam Dix scolded her.

Dorothea cried. She thought that she would never please her grandmother.

Before long, Madam Dix decided that she needed help. She asked her sister Sarah and Sarah's daughter, Mrs. Sarah Fiske, for advice. "Maybe I am too old to train the girl," she said.

They were very understanding. "Let Dorothea come to us in Worcester for a few years," they said.

Mrs. Fiske added, "I will treat her like my own daughter."

Madam Dix decided to send Dorothea to Worcester. Dorothea's many relatives greeted her warmly. "My, how pretty you are," Mrs. Fiske said. This pleased Dorothea. Nobody had ever called her pretty before.

The two ladies were kind and patient. Soon Dorothea settled down. By the time she was fourteen, she could sew and cook almost as well as her cousin. "Your grandmother will be pleased with you, Dorothea," Mrs. Fiske said.

Dorothea had fun too. She had many cousins in Worcester.

They were all kind to her. She went walking and skating with the girls.

One family of cousins, the Wheelers, invited her to visit them every Sunday afternoon. Their two little daughters, Nancy and Frances, liked Dorothea at once. "Tell us a story, Cousin Dolly," they begged.

One day as she talked to them, she heard someone say, "You are a born teacher."

She looked up to see a tall, fair-haired young man standing before her.

"Cousin Edward!" Nancy exclaimed.

Dorothea knew this must be her cousin, Edward Bangs. He was the son of Judge Bangs. Edward, a lawyer, had just returned from a trip south. At 28, he seemed very grown-up to Dorothea.

"So this is Dorothea Lynde Dix," he said, smiling. He seemed interested in her and asked questions about Boston. When he left, little Frances said, "Isn't he handsome, Cousin Dolly?" Dorothea agreed.

She saw Edward Bangs often after that. He began to meet her on Sunday afternoons as she walked to the Wheelers. They became good friends. Dorothea's other cousins began to tease her about her "beau."

Chapter *4*

First School

Telling stories to her young cousins gave Dorothea an idea. She would start a school. In those days, teachers were very young.

Mrs. Fiske protested. "But you don't have to teach. Your grandfather left money for you. You will have it when you are 21."

"That is too long to wait!" Dorothea said. "I need money now so I can send for my brothers. They must have a better life. My parents will let them come."

Mrs. Fiske nodded. "The boys can live with us."

"Oh, thank you!" Dorothea exclaimed. "But what about my school, Cousin Sarah? May I start one?"

Mrs. Fiske smiled. "We will speak to Judge Bangs."

Dorothea had to wait until her cousins approved of her plan. Finally, they did. Edward Bangs rented an empty store on Main Street for the school.

The first day, Dorothea waited nervously for pupils to come. She had pinned up her hair and lengthened her skirts. She would be very strict. Then her pupils would not guess she was only fourteen.

"Good morning, Miss Dix!" Two little boys had popped their heads in the doorway, grinning.

Miss Dix! It had a grown-up sound. She knew the boys. "William and Levi Lincoln, you may sit in the first row."

Frances and Nancy Wheeler came next, then Joseph Eaton, Anne Bancroft, and Lucy Green. The very best families in Worcester were sending their children to Dorothea's school. When her brothers arrived, they were pupils too.

Dorothea taught the children reading, writing, and manners. Each one had to learn a chapter from the Bible every week and say it on Monday morning.

Miss Dix was firm but fair. She punished the children when they were naughty. She was especially strict with her own brothers.

William Lincoln was always getting into mischief.

One day Dorothea turned around to see him pulling Lucy Green's long hair. "William Lincoln, you are an imp," she said. "I must spank you again today."

Only the boys were spanked. The little girls were punished in other ways. Once Nancy Wheeler forgot to learn her Bible lesson. She had to wear a sign around her neck. The sign said, "A very bad girl indeed."

Dorothea loved teaching. She kept her school until she was seventeen. Then her grandmother sent for her, and she returned to Boston. Her brothers stayed in Worcester with Cousin Sarah Fiske. Later, they too went to Orange Court to live. Madam Dix sent them to good schools in Boston.

Chapter 5

A Busy Life

Madam Dix was pleased when she saw how attractive Dorothea had become.

"It is time for you to think about marriage," Madam Dix told her.

Dorothea knew that Edward Bangs was in love with her. She had promised to write to him and let him visit her in Boston. But she was not ready for marriage. There was so much she wanted to learn first. "I want to study some more," she told Grandmother.

In those days, women did not go to college. So Dorothea went to lectures and read books in the public library.

She learned about the famous preacher, Dr. William Channing. One Sunday, she went to his church to hear him. His goodness and kindness showed in every word he spoke. "The poor and the handicapped need our help," he said.

Dorothea kept going to hear Dr. Channing. One Sunday after the service, a pretty, dark-haired girl came up to her.

"We should know each other," the girl said. "I have seen you here often. I am Ann Heath, from Brookline."

Dorothea smiled. She liked the girl's friendliness. "I am Dorothea Lynde Dix."

"Isn't Dr. Channing wonderful?" Ann said.

"Oh, yes!" Dorothea replied. "If only I could do as he says and help others."

"I am sure you will," Ann said. "As for me, I must stay home and look after my family. Won't you come and visit?"

"I would love to," Dorothea said.

She and Ann became good friends. Dorothea liked the large, lively Heath family. "I always hate to leave your house," she told Ann.

After a few years Dorothea was ready to start teaching again. She asked her grandmother if she could have a girls' school in Orange Court.

Madam Dix did not like the idea of a school in her own house. "My carpets! My furniture!" she cried.

But as usual, Dorothea had her way. She opened a second school, too, for poor children. This she held in the mornings, in the carriage house. Besides the schools, Dorothea managed the household for her grandmother. She also kept on with her own studies.

When her father died, she worked even harder to forget the sadness of her childhood. She saw that her mother was taken care of in a nursing home. Her brother Charles went to sea and became a sailor. Joseph went into business.

Dorothea's schools ran like clockwork. There was a time for everything. The girls especially loved the nature walks Miss Dix took with them almost every afternoon. The girls were very fond of their teacher.

She wrote a book, based on her nature talks. She called it *Conversations on Common Things*. The book was very popular. She went on to write other tales and poems for children.

Dorothea's life was so full that she could not think of marriage. Edward Bangs got tired of waiting for her. He married someone else.

At first Dorothea was upset. She would not talk about Edward and she destroyed all of his letters. Later, she realized that her work and her friends brought her true happiness.

Dorothea and Ann Heath got to know Dr. Channing well. They visited him and his family in their Boston home. Dr. Channing became interested in Dorothea's work, especially her schools.

"But you are working too hard," he said. "You will ruin your health."

Dorothea admitted that she had a pain in her chest.

"Come with us to the seashore for the summer," Dr. Channing said. "You can be our children's governess and have a chance to rest too."

Dorothea was delighted. Later, the Channings asked her to go with them to an island in the Caribbean. They spent six months there. Dorothea rested and became well.

When she returned to Boston, she worked just as hard as before. In a few years she was sick again.

"You have lung trouble," her doctor told her. "You must stop teaching and go to a warmer place to live."

Dr. Channing came to see her and agreed. "Go to Italy for the winter," he said. "But first, stop in England and visit my friends, the Rathbones."

Dorothea was sorry she had to close her schools. But she had always wanted to travel abroad. She was glad when Madam Dix encouraged her to go on a long trip.

Chapter 6

New Ideas

Dorothea's ship sailed for Europe in April, 1836. The Atlantic was stormy. Most of the passengers were seasick. After six weeks they landed in Liverpool, England. Dorothea was so weak that she had to go to bed in her hotel.

The next morning, Dr. Channing's friends, the Rathbones, came to the hotel to see her. She was very ill.

"You are coming home with us, to Greenbank," said kind Mrs. Rathbone. "You need care and rest."

"But you do not even know me," Dorothea whispered.

"It is enough for us that you are Dr. Channing's friend," Mr. Rathbone said.

She expected to stay only a short time with her new friends. She never dreamed it would be eighteen months before she was well enough to leave. All that time the Rathbones looked after her. They were the kindest people Dorothea had ever known.

Mr. Rathbone was a rich merchant. He spent a great deal of time and money helping others. Many friends came to visit him at Greenbank.

One of the visitors Dorothea liked best was a gentle Quaker named Samuel Tuke. He was the doctor in charge of York Retreat, a home for insane people.

In those days, mentally ill people were called "insane."

"The insane must be treated as sick people," Dr. Tuke said, "not as criminals or wild animals." He explained that in ancient times, people thought insanity was caused by evil spirits. Later, insane persons were shut away, sometimes in dungeons.

"Now," Dr. Tuke said, "there are a few hospitals that treat insanity as an illness. But only the rich can afford these hospitals. The poor are kept in jails and workhouses. Most of the time they are forgotten."

His angry eyes blazed as he went on. "Mental illness can be cured! We must make people see that it is an illness, not a crime."

Dorothea began to be excited by Dr. Tuke's ideas.

Bad news, however, came from home. First her mother died. Before Dorothea was well enough to travel, word came that Madam Dix had died too.

Sadly, Dorothea wrote to Ann Heath, "There is no need to hurry home now."

She stayed at Greenbank until she was entirely well. Then in the fall of 1837, she said good-bye to her English friends.

"You have given me back my health," she told them. "I will never forget you."

The Rathbones gave her something else too. Now she was certain that she wanted to spend the rest of her life helping others.

Chapter 7

Life Work

When Dorothea returned to Boston, some of her cousins were cool to her. They thought she should have been with Madam Dix during her last illness. Dorothea was hurt—and lonely. Orange Court was closed, so she lived in a boarding house. Her health would not allow her to teach. She was 36. It seemed that her best years were over.

She visited orphan homes and wrote more stories for children. But she was not satisfied.

She was looking for a "cause." She wanted a big job that would take all of her time and skill.

She found it on a rainy day in 1841.

A young man named John Nichols came to see her at her boarding house. "I hope you can help me, Miss Dix," he said.

John Nichols was studying to be a minister. He was looking for a Sunday school teacher for the women prisoners in the East Cambridge Jail.

"It is not a pleasant place," he said. "Many ladies would be afraid. Could you suggest someone, Miss Dix?"

Dorothea nodded. "Yes. I can surely suggest someone—myself."

"Oh! But I have heard that you are in poor health," Mr. Nichols said.

"I shall be there next Sunday," Dorothea said firmly.

The following Sunday, she faced a roomful of ragged women prisoners. She spoke softly and read to them in her low, beautiful voice. The restless women became quiet. Dorothea told them she would come back the next week.

Before she left, she walked through the jail.

There was one door the jailer would not open. "That's where insane people are kept," he said.

"I would like to see them."

"Why, Ma'am, you couldn't stand it!"

"Please open the door," Dorothea insisted.

"Well, don't say I didn't warn you," he grumbled. He unlocked the door.

Dorothea walked into a room that was bitterly cold and damp. The air was bad. The noise made her want to cover her ears. Several women in rags huddled together for warmth. A few sobbed and cried. Dorothea walked around and spoke to them. She held their cold hands. Her heart was touched by the sad sight.

"These poor creatures will never get well here," she told the jailer.

He stared at her. "The insane don't get well," he said.

"At least give them a little heat," she continued.

He shook his head. "They don't feel the cold."

Dorothea decided something must be done. She went to the town council.

The men on the council did not want to hear about the insane people in the jail. They even said she was a busybody.

"What shall I do?" she asked Dr. Channing.

"I am sure that Dr. Samuel Howe and Charles Sumner will help you," he said. "You must go to them."

Both of these famous men listened to Dorothea. Then they visited the jail and saw that she had spoken the truth. They wrote to the newspapers. They got people interested in conditions in the jail. At last, the town council did something. They provided heat for the insane people.

It was a small victory but it was important. It started Dorothea on her life work for the mentally ill.

Before, no one had spoken up for these poor forgotten people in public institutions. Dorothea Lynde Dix would. She worked the rest of her life to improve their care and treatment.

Chapter *8*

Famous Woman

For two years, Dorothea visited the jails in Massachusetts. She found some mentally ill people in every jail. They were treated far worse than criminals.

She wrote a report of what she had seen. She sent it to the state legislature where the laws were made. She knew now that the best way to work for her cause was through the state government.

In the report, Dorothea told about the mentally ill people she had seen locked in cages, closets, and pens. She had seen them chained and beaten.

The report was made public. It was like a big bombshell exploding. People became angry, but for different reasons. Some people were angry because the state let such things happen. Many more were angry because they thought the report was not true.

Dorothea's friends, however, believed it. Dr. Channing, Dr. Howe, and the well-known educator, Horace Mann, all encouraged her. They helped to get a law passed to make the State Hospital at Worcester bigger. All mentally ill people in the state could go there.

This was Dorothea's first big success.

She went on to Connecticut and Rhode Island. She found the same kinds of conditions there. In Rhode Island she found an insane man chained in a stone cell. The room had no light or fresh air. She asked some of the rich people in the state to give money for a hospital for the insane. A man named Cyrus Butler was on her list.

"He is a hard man to part from his money," friends told her.

In Mr. Butler's office, Dorothea went straight to the point. "Mr. Butler, I want you to give $40,000 to enlarge the State Hospital in Providence."

He looked hard at this small, ladylike person. She wore a dark dress and her hair was plainly arranged. Yet she was beautiful. Her eyes were shining.

"Miss Dix," Cyrus Butler said. "I have heard of you, and I was ready to turn you down. But you are not the kind of person I expected. I have changed my mind. I'll give the money if a like amount is given by others."

Dorothea agreed. In a short time she had his check. People called her "the marvel of Rhode Island."

Then she went on to New Jersey. There was no hospital for the insane in the entire state. Dorothea lived in a boarding house in Trenton, near the state capitol. Every evening, for weeks, she talked to the state legislators in her parlor. She told them about the sad cases she had seen in New Jersey. She asked them to pass a law for a state hospital.

They listened, but for a long time they did not help her. One evening, the leader of the men got up. "You have won me over," he said. "The Lord bless you, Miss Dix!"

Dorothea helped to pick out a place for the New Jersey State Hospital at Trenton. She helped to plan its design. She called this hospital her "first child." It always had a special place in her heart.

Dorothea went on to other states— Pennsylvania, Ohio, and Illinois. She traveled in all kinds of weather. She went by wagon, stagecoach, and river boat. Sometimes there were long delays. She used the time to read more and more about the latest treatment for mental illness.

In North Carolina she nursed a dying woman in her hotel. She stayed with the woman to the end. Afterward, the woman's husband came to her. Tears were running down his face.

"Miss Dix, my wife's last request was to help you get your law passed. I will do everything in my power."

He was one of the most important men in the state legislature!

Soon a hospital for the insane was built in North Carolina. Dorothea was told it would be named Dix Hill, for her.

"Not for me," she said, "but for my grandfather, Dr. Elijah Dix."

Her fame was growing. She received letters from all over the country asking for her help.

"I must go," she told Ann Heath. Soon she was on her way to Louisiana, Alabama, Georgia, and South Carolina.

Once her stagecoach was held up by a robber. She leaned out the window to ask what was wrong. The masked man heard her.

"That voice!" he said. "I remember! You are Miss Dix. You spoke to my mother in a hospital in Pennsylvania." Then he shouted to the driver. "Go on! I won't take money from anyone in Miss Dix's company."

Dorothea Dix helped the cause of the mentally ill in every state she visited.

Then a new dream began to form in her mind. The national as well as the state governments should help! Such help would be much greater.

At that time, there were vast empty lands out in the West. The government owned them all. Dorothea wanted the government to sell some of the land. It could use the money to build hospitals for the insane.

It was a long, hard struggle to get Congressmen and Senators on her side. She stayed in Washington, D.C., for four years, talking about and pleading for her land bill. At last, it was passed by both houses of Congress.

The bill was sent to President Pierce. It could not become law without his signature. But the President refused to sign the bill! He said this law would let the states turn over their jobs to the government. The states should care for their own poor and handicapped, he said.

Dorothea was heartbroken. She felt that her years of work were lost. The law she wanted so much was never passed.

Dorothea went abroad for a long rest. She visited the Rathbones at Greenbank again. Her name was known now all over Europe. She was asked by many countries to visit their hospitals. Soon she was traveling from one to the other. She gave advice to others, but she also learned much too. Many hospitals in Europe were ahead of America in caring for their mentally ill people.

Dorothea spent two years abroad. Then she returned to America ready for more work.

Chapter 9

Civil War Nurse

The next four years were very busy ones for Dorothea. She told Ann Heath, "The more I do for the mentally sick and the poor, the more I see to do." She helped to start the Hospital for the Insane of the Army and Navy in Washington, D. C. This is now called St. Elizabeth's Hospital. There were many fiery speeches in Congress in Washington at this time. The North and South were quarreling over slavery. Many people felt sure that war was coming.

Dorothea kept on with her work, still hoping that war could be avoided. Though she was against slavery, she traveled through the South raising money for more hospitals there. "My job is to help the insane, both North and South," she said.

In November, 1860, Abraham Lincoln was elected President. The Southerners knew Lincoln would not allow slavery to spread. Soon after his election, South Carolina left the Union. Other Southern states joined her. They claimed that they were a new nation, the Confederate States of America.

There was no fighting, however. Then in April, 1861, Southern troops fired on Fort Sumter. President Lincoln called for soldiers to put down the rebellion.

Dorothea was in Trenton visiting the Trenton State Hospital.

"This means civil war," she said when she read the newspaper.

Two regiments of Massachusetts troops started on their way to Washington. They were attacked by a large mob in Baltimore.

Dorothea heard the news. "I must take the next train south," she said. "There will be wounded to care for."

She went to Washington and offered her services to the War Department. The Secretary of War accepted her offer at once. He made her Superintendent of United States Army Nurses. Her job was to choose nurses for the Union Army. Soon, she would be in charge of the nurses in all the army hospitals.

Many women came to Washington wanting to be army nurses. At that time, there were no schools for trained nurses in any hospitals. Dorothea Dix was not a trained nurse. She knew more about hospitals, however, than almost any other woman in the country. She also knew what kind of nurses she wanted.

"An army hospital is no place for a girl or woman who does not have good health, courage, and character," she said. "No woman under 30 need apply. All nurses should be plain in dress, with no curls, no jewelry, and no hoopskirts." Her first question to those who came was, "Are you ready to work?"

Dorothea herself worked for four long years without a vacation.

She fought disease, carelessness, and dirt. Through her, nursing standards in all hospitals were raised. Dorothea also fought some of the army doctors. She told them whenever she found anything wrong in their hospitals. They did not like this. So they complained to the Secretary of War, but he always backed Dorothea.

One day she inspected a hospital near Washington. She pointed out the dirt, the bad food, and the lack of comfort for the sick and wounded soldiers. The doctor was cross. "Madam, who are you to tell me, the officer in charge?"

Dorothea drew herself up to her full height. She said proudly, "I am Dorothea L. Dix, Superintendent of Nurses, in the employ of the United States."

To the suffering men in the hospitals, she was an angel of mercy. She brought them fruit and jellies. She smoothed their pillows and wrote letters for them. Sadly, she sent for relatives when she saw that a soldier was dying.

"This war in my own country is breaking my heart," she wrote to Mrs. Rathbone.

In 1862, a tall, brown-haired young woman came to Washington. She asked Miss Dix if she could be an army nurse. She was Louisa May Alcott, who was to become famous later as the author of *Little Women*.

Dorothea liked her plain, sensible look and her willingness to work. She sent Louisa to the Union Hotel, which had been turned into a hospital.

The young woman worked very hard at her job. Then, after only six weeks, she got pneumonia. Dorothea ordered her to go home.

"Please let me stay," Louisa begged. "I'm sure I will be better soon."

Instead she grew worse. Dorothea sent for Mr. Alcott to come for his daughter. Sadly, Louisa left Washington. Later she wrote about her experiences in a book called *Hospital Sketches*.

At last a day came when shouts and music filled the air. Robert E. Lee, the Confederate general, had surrendered.

That night, the lights in the city of Washington burned brightly. Dorothea went to her window and watched the happy, singing crowds. She thanked God the war was over.

Chapter *10*

Later Years

Dorothea stayed on in Washington during the long, hot summer. There were still wounded soldiers to nurse. She was also trying to get pensions for nurses who were not well. Some had become sick through their war service.

At last Dorothea returned home to Massachusetts. There she stayed with Ann Heath for a while. Then she visited her brother Joseph and his family.

"Are you ready to retire now, Dolly?" Joseph asked.

Dorothea shook her head. "No indeed. I am going to take up my work again." She smiled. "My real work."

Joseph nodded. He knew that his sister's work for the insane was closest to her heart.

At 65, Dorothea was lively and quick. She looked younger than her age. Soon she was traveling again. She inspected all kinds of places where the mentally ill were kept. She pointed out the need for more hospitals. The war had broken the minds and spirits of many soldiers.

Many of the hospitals for the insane had become run-down during the war years. New hospitals had to be built, and old ones made bigger. Dorothea went from Maine to Florida, from New York to California.

She worked for fifteen more years. She became known and loved by many. Dorothea was recognized everywhere— a little old lady in a dark dress, bonnet, and shawl. She never had to pay fares on trains or ships. Railroad presidents and owners of steamship lines sent her free passes.

She helped many charities. Always, she was collecting food, clothing, and other things for needy groups. Children were named for her. Hospitals which she had started hung her picture on their walls.

Dorothea Dix was nearly 80 years old when she finally retired. She became ill and went to the Trenton State Hospital to live. She had a sunny apartment where she could see the Delaware River.

Here, she entertained her friends. This is where Dorothea spent her last years.

Dorothea Lynde Dix will always be remembered as a pioneer in providing for the insane. She took up the cause of the most hopeless and neglected people in America. Her courage and devotion to her cause brought about better treatment for the mentally ill, fine hospitals, and above all—hope.